# MOSES
# 10 Plagues

Ex. 1:6—12:36 for Children

Written by Connie Hodges
Illustrated by Jules Edler

**ARCH® Books**

Copyright © 1985 CONCORDIA PUBLISHING HOUSE
3558 S. Jefferson Avenue, St. Louis, MO 63118-3968
Manufactured in the United States of America

Long before God's people lived
Within the Promised Land,
They lived in Egypt—welcomed guests
By Pharaoh's command.

But then another Pharaoh
Arose. He was afraid
The Hebrew clans would grow and be
his enemies one day.

"They'll leave my land; they'll leave my rule;
Their loss would be a pity!
I'll turn them into slaves for me
And make them build my cities."

The Hebrew cries went up to God;
He heard their sore desire.
He spoke to Moses and He said
(from in a bush on fire):

"Take these My words to Pharaoh
For he is now My foe:
'I've come to rescue Israel,
So let My people go!' "

"I do not know your Hebrew God,
So, NO!" said Pharaoh.
"Ha! Go and make the bricks we need
And do not be so slow!"

Then Moses did a miracle—
Done by the power of God—
The Nile River turned to blood
When hit with Moses' rod.

The fish all died, the river smelled
As bad as it could be.
But still the heart of Pharaoh
Refused to set them free.

Time went by, but nothing changed.
God's voice was soft and low:
"I'll send the king a plague of frogs
If he won't let you go.

"Frogs and more frogs, tell the king,
Will jump into his home,
In ovens, bowls, and on his bed,
All over will they roam."

But, when the frogs were gone, the heart
Of Pharaoh was ice.
So God sent yet another plague,
This time a plague of lice.

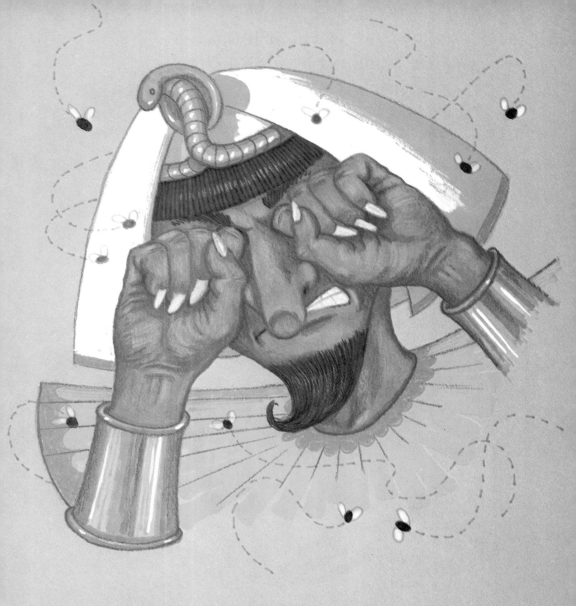

When Pharaoh refused to budge
God sent the fourth plague: Flies—
Flies that flew through everything,
In people's hair and eyes.

The heart of Pharaoh was cold,
He would not lose this battle.
So God sent still another plague:
Black death to Egypt's cattle.

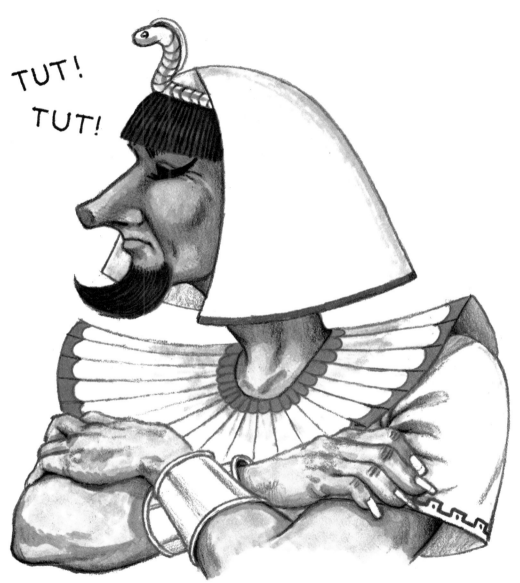

Though this was seen by Pharaoh,
His heart was very slow
To bow to Moses and to God,
To let God's people go.

So Moses gathered ashes up
And spread them in the air.
And when the dust had settled down,
Sores broke out everywhere.

Then God sent hail and fire
And locusts flying low;
But nothing that the Lord would send
Would change this Pharaoh.

Then darkness covered Egypt's land,
So thick it could be felt;
But Pharaoh refused to change
The awful way he dealt.

"The firstborn in the land will die,"
Said God, "That's *every* one.
Tonight the king will feel *this* plague—
He has a firstborn son."

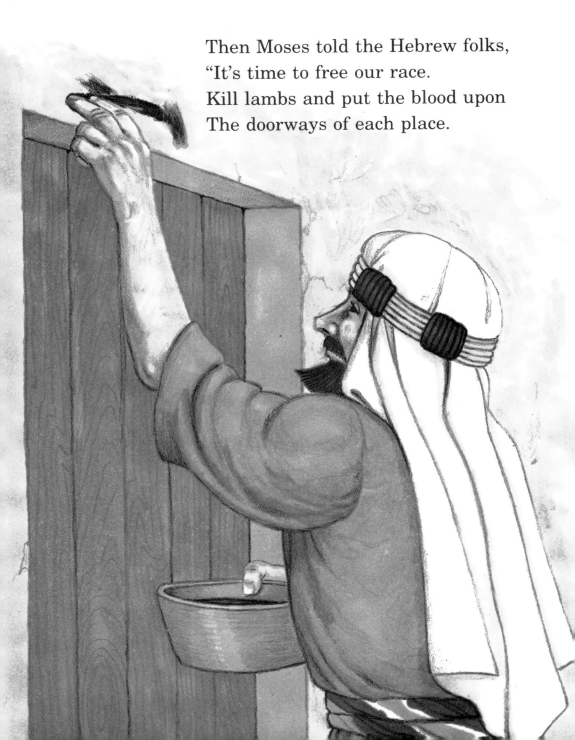

Then Moses told the Hebrew folks,
"It's time to free our race.
Kill lambs and put the blood upon
The doorways of each place.

"Next, roast a lamb and on its meat
Use herbs, and bake some bread.
Stay in your homes till morning comes;
You've nothing, friends, to dread."

Amid the darkest part of night
The angel Death, alone,
Appeared to take the firstborn son
Of each Egyptian home.

When Pharaoh arose to find
His own son, too, had died,
He grieved, "I've lost. And God is God.
Bring Moses to my side.

"Worship God the way you will.
Take flocks and herds along.
Leave this land, soon as you can,
Before we all are gone."

That night they fled from Pharaoh;
Their faith was in their God
Who freed them from their slavery
Through Moses' mighty rod.

## DEAR PARENTS

The exciting story of the Exodus from Egypt belongs to Jews and Christians alike. If God had not brought the Hebrews out from their slavery, the entire history of humanity would have been different.

The Lord freed the Hebrews from their oppression both because He was grieved by their suffering and because He was faithful to the promises He had given to them through their ancestors, Abraham, Isaac, and Jacob. God had a special plan for the Hebrew people. Through their history God's saving will and love was to become known to humanity. In Jesus Christ, a son of the Hebrew people, Abraham's family became a blessing to all the earth.

The story of the Exodus is also a story of the power of God over the power of evil. When faced with seemingly insurmountable problems, young children (as well as many adults) wonder if God truly cares about them and is able to help them. The story of the Hebrews in Egypt and their deliverance reminds us that God does not forget His plans for our good, even though after 430 years (Ex. 12:40) it may have seemed so to the Hebrews. Nor can the greatest power on earth prevent the Almighty One from accomplishing His will.

As you read this story with your children, help them focus on this greatness of God's concern and love for His people, including your children. They are His through Jesus, who delivered them from slavery to sin through His death and resurrection.

THE EDITOR